Amy R. Murray, M. Ed.

with illustrations by David L. Barber

National Center for Youth Issues

Practical Guidance Resources
Educators Can Trust

P.O. Box 22185 • Chattanooga, TN 37422-2185
423.899.5714 • 800.477.8277
fax: 423.899.4547 • www.ncyi.org

National Center for Youth Issues
Practical Guidance Resources
Educators Can Trust

P.O. Box 22185
Chattanooga, TN 37422-2185
423.899.5714 • 800.477.8277
fax: 423.899.4547
www.ncyi.org

ISBN: (13-digit) 978-1-931636-71-1, (10-digit) 1-931636-71-0

© 2006 National Center for Youth Issues, Chattanooga, TN
All rights reserved.

Written by: Amy R. Murray, M. Ed.
Cover Design and Page Layout by: Phillip W. Rodgers
Illustrations by Contract: David L. Barber
Published by National Center for Youth Issues

Printed in the United States of America

Dedication

This book is dedicated to the students
of Windsor Hill Elementary School
who we loved and lost.

Acknowledgment

With much gratitude to Janet Bender,
my colleague and friend of more than twenty years,
who invited me to write a book with her and then
continued to inspire and encourage me to write.

Introduction

Grief. Grief is difficult, yet something that everybody has to experience at one time or another. Grief is a part of life, though something we would like to avoid. Like all societal issues, grief eventually comes to school. What do we do when a school is grief stricken? This book is written to help school counselors, teachers, and administrators know how to respond when grief affects a school.

I will never forget that Friday in March 2005. It had been an ordinary day, and I was looking forward to the weekend. Just as I was walking through the office at the end of the day, a co-op student asked me to pick up the phone. It was someone at the transportation office she said, and it was urgent. I took a deep breath, said a quick prayer, and picked up the phone. After the voice on the line had me identify myself as the school counselor, I heard, "One of the bus drivers just ran over a student…he's frantic…EMS has been called…but can you go to the neighborhood?" Of course, I went, taking the school nurse with me.

The worst of course had happened….the student died from the accident. Our school was overcome with grief. Thank goodness, I was not the only counselor. Together, Bill Ryland and I made it through the next couple of weeks, helping students, teachers, parents, and administrators cope with the loss. Helping others grieve when you are grieving yourself is very difficult. It certainly would have been helpful to have had a grief recovery resource at my fingertips. Thus, the idea for this book was born.

I hope that your school does not have to experience the sudden or expected loss of a student, staff, or family member. However, if your school does experience such a loss, hopefully this book will help guide you through the grief process while helping others.

Amy R. Murray, M. Ed.

Table of Contents

Mending Hearts

Tools for School Staff and Parents

When a Tragic Loss Occurs
(Crisis Team Checklist)

✓ **What to do first:**

- As soon as possible, gather the school crisis team (counselors, nurse, teachers, and administrators) together.

- As a team, decide what needs to be done immediately.

- Develop a plan for how to respond over the next two days.

- Assign tasks to team members.

✓ **How to respond:**

- Response needs to be made as quickly as possible, either that day or the next.

- Make sure those people closest to the situation are given information, sparing them unnecessary details.

- In structured settings, allow people to share their feelings and concerns. (You may need to ask counselors from other schools to assist you.)

- Identify those persons who will need more intense counseling help.

✓ **Ways to provide support:**

- As soon as possible, speak to the faculty to give information about what occurred and explain how they can help. Allow them to share their feelings.

- As soon as possible, speak to the group of students most affected by the loss. Explain briefly what happened without giving unnecessary details. Give students a chance to share their feelings. (Having another person with you can be very helpful; someone to observe the class and look for high-risk students.)

- Have designated rooms in the building where high-risk students can go to talk to counselors one-on-one.

- Get students to draw or write about the loss. Often students are more comfortable expressing themselves in this way.

- Decide on a "Remembrance" spot in the hall, or make a banner, where cards, pictures, and tributes to the person may be hung.

- Give teachers and parents involved the age-appropriate "Mending Hearts" handouts pages, so they will know how they can help students experiencing loss.

Helping 3-5 Year-olds

As parents and teachers we want to protect our children from pain, fear, and sadness. But sheltering them from the pain of death can do more harm than good. If parents and teachers are uncomfortable talking about death and hide their own feelings, children may learn it's a taboo subject and not ask questions they may have. It's important to encourage children to express their grief and to see you doing the same.

We hope that the following information will help you talk to your children.

Helping 3-5 Year-olds

1. A typical preschooler thinks death is reversible as seen on television and in movies. State the reality of death without giving too much information. Repeat the facts calmly and simply—when someone dies his body doesn't work anymore. When someone dies he can't come alive again.

2. Preschoolers have a fuzzy concept of death. Don't describe dying as falling or going to sleep and never waking up. You may cause the child to start having sleep problems.

To Help Children of All Ages

1. Make your explanation of death brief. Keep the information factual, simple, and honest.

2. Focus on feelings. Let children know that most if not all of their feelings are perfectly natural and normal. Do not tell children how they should feel.

3. Children may need to ask the same questions over and over. Be patient with them and answer their questions without going into too much detail.

4. Help them develop a sense of closure about the loss. Help them remember special moments they shared with the person who died. Encourage them to draw pictures or write about special moments.

5. Maintain order and stability by keeping routines as much as possible.

Adapted in part from <u>Losing a Loved One: Helping Children Grieve.</u> Parents magazine, July 2001.

Mending Hearts
When a school grieves

Helping 6-7 Year-olds

As parents and teachers we want to protect our children from pain, fear, and sadness. But sheltering them from the pain of death can do more harm than good. If parents and teachers are uncomfortable talking about death and hide their own feelings, children may learn it's a taboo subject and not ask questions they may have. It's important to encourage children to express their grief and to see you doing the same.

We hope that the following information will help you talk to your children.

Helping 6-7 Year-olds

1. Children this age understand they can die. They fear death. Their talk can be fearful and they need lots of reassurance.

2. Children this age are usually able to understand that death is permanent. They want to see lots of pictures and talk frequently about the person who died. This behavior may last for as long as a year.

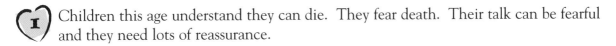

To Help Children of All Ages

1. Make your explanation of death brief. Keep the information factual, simple, and honest.

2. Focus on feelings. Let children know that most if not all of their feelings are perfectly natural and normal. Do not tell children how they should feel.

3. Children may need to ask the same questions over and over. Be patient with them and answer their questions without going into too much detail.

4. Help them develop a sense of closure about the loss. Help them remember special moments they shared with the person who died. Encourage them to draw pictures or write about special moments.

5. Maintain order and stability by keeping routines as much as possible.

Adapted in part from <u>Losing a Loved One: Helping Children Grieve.</u> *Parents magazine, July 2001.*

Helping 8-10 Year-olds

As parents and teachers we want to protect our children from pain, fear, and sadness. But sheltering them from the pain of death can do more harm than good. If parents and teachers are uncomfortable talking about death and hide their own feelings, children may learn it's a taboo subject and not ask questions they may have. It's important to encourage children to express their grief and to see you doing the same.

We hope that the following information will help you talk to your children.

Helping 8-10 Year-olds

1 Children this age understand that death is final.

2 They may express concern about the effect of death on them with regards to lifestyle or finances. They are more future oriented.

3 Children this age may have a flippant attitude. This attitude is a defense mechanism. Children might try to avoid their true feelings because they fear acknowledging them would cause them to loose control. Children this age, especially boys, do not want to look weak in the eyes of their friends.

4 Children this age may feel more comfortable writing down their feelings or drawing pictures. You can also tell them that if they decide to talk about feelings, you will be glad to listen.

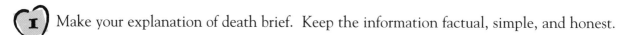

To Help Children of All Ages

1 Make your explanation of death brief. Keep the information factual, simple, and honest.

2 Focus on feelings. Let children know that most if not all of their feelings are perfectly natural and normal. Do not tell children how they should feel.

3 Children may need to ask the same questions over and over. Be patient with them and answer their questions without going into too much detail.

4 Help them develop a sense of closure about the loss. Remember special moments they shared with the person who died. Encourage them to draw pictures or write about special moments.

5 Maintain order and stability by keeping routines as much as possible

Adapted in part from Losing a Loved One: Helping Children Grieve. *Parents magazine, July 2001.*

Mending Hearts
When a school grieves

Helping 11-13 Year-olds

As parents and teachers we want to protect our children from pain, fear, and sadness. But sheltering them from the pain of death can do more harm than good. If parents and teachers are uncomfortable talking about death and hide their own feelings, children may learn it's a taboo subject and not ask questions they may have. It's important to encourage children to express their grief and to see you doing the same.

We hope that the following information will help you talk to your children.

Helping 11-13 Year-olds

1 Children this age may appear self-centered. They want to figure out how this death may change their lives.

2 Children in this age group are interested in more detailed information about why the person died, because it helps them feel more in control.

3 Children this age have a more realistic view of death. There may be curiosity about the biological aspects of death.

To Help Children of All Ages

1 Make your explanation of death brief. Keep the information factual, simple, and honest.

2 Focus on feelings. Let children know that most if not all of their feelings are perfectly natural and normal. Do not tell children how they should feel.

3 Children may need to ask the same questions over and over. Be patient with them and answer their questions without going into too much detail.

4 Help them develop a sense of closure about the loss. Help them to remember special moments they shared with the person who died. Encourage them to draw pictures or write about special moments.

5 Maintain order and stability by keeping routines as much as possible.

Adapted in part from <u>Losing a Loved One: Helping Children Grieve.</u> *Parents magazine, July 2001.*

Mending Hearts

Understanding the Stages of Grief

Mending Hearts through the Stages of Grief

The grief process involves moving through the following stages
as described by Elizabeth Kubler-Ross.
People move back and forth through these stages in different orders.

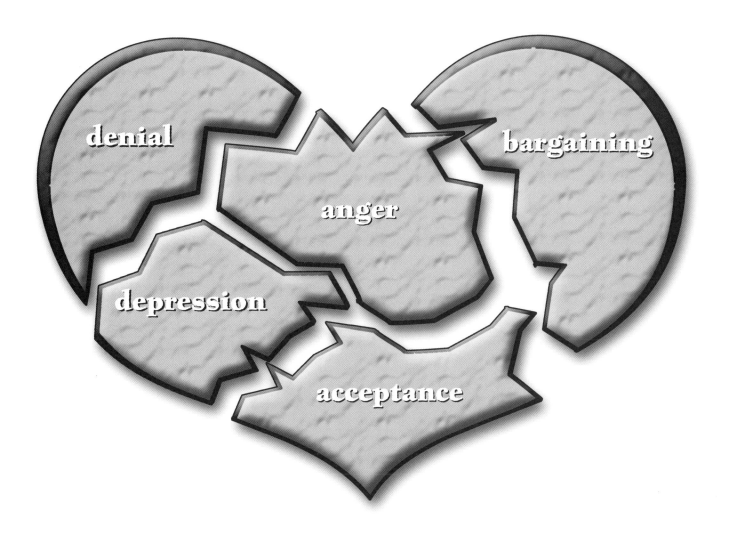

Mending Hearts
When a school grieves

The Five Stages of Grief

The five stages of grief (Kubler-Ross, 1997) provide suggestions for dealing with the uncomfortable and painful situation surrounding the death of a loved one. After moving through all the stages, acceptance of death is achieved.

Denial
By denying that something happened we buffer ourselves from the painful news for awhile. This is usually a temporary defense mechanism.

Anger
Anger replaces denial. Feelings of anger, rage, envy, and resentment may be projected onto people and situations almost at random.

Bargaining
Usually bargaining takes place only for very brief periods. An agreement with God or self is made, which attempts to postpone the inevitable.

Depression
A great sense of loss sets in as a person tries to accept permanent separation. Expressing sadness and grief is very important. This stage may linger quite awhile.

Acceptance
Mourning the loss is complete. Previous feelings have all been expressed.

Mending Hearts
When a school grieves

Talking to Kids About Grief
Dos and Don'ts of Communication

Dos...

1. Give facts in a simple manner.

2. Allow children to ask questions.

3. Share your feelings.

4. Listen carefully as children share their feelings.

5. Appropriate statements to use are:
   - "I'm sorry."
   - "I care."
   - "I'm here for you."
   - "I want to help you."
   - "You feel _____, because _____."
   - "All your feelings are okay."

Don'ts...

1. Don't give children more information than they ask for.

2. Don't tell children to just give it time.

3. Don't encourage children to ignore their feelings or to try not to think about it.

4. Don't say any of the following:
   - "It is a blessing."
   - "She's in a better place."
   - "At least he didn't suffer."
   - "Be glad you had her as long as you did."
   - "You'll be stronger because of this."
   - Don't say anything that could minimize the child's loss.

Adapted in part from Wolfelt, Alan D. (1998). Healing The Grieving Heart: 100 Practical Ideas for Families, Friends, and Caregivers. Fort Collins, Colorado: Companion Press.

© National Center for Youth Issues • www.ncyi.org
Please refer to page 2 for duplication and copyright information

Mending Hearts
when a school grieves

19

Mending Hearts
When a school grieves

A Story for Children

by

Amy R. Murray, M. Ed.

with illustrations by David L. Barber

At our school every student is special and important.

Here are the names of the students in my class.

_____   _____   _____

_____   _____   _____

_____   _____   _____

_____   _____   _____

_____   _____   _____

_____   _____   _____

Here is a picture(s) of my best friend(s) in class.

Please paste pictures here.

A class is like a family. We all help one another, and care about each other. How do you feel about your class?

_____

_____

One school day a classmate was absent. We thought Jimmy was sick, but our teacher looked very sad.

Mending Hearts
When a school grieves

The counselor came to talk to us. She said that Jimmy had died in a bus accident. She said that Jimmy was gone forever, and would not be back.

Some students began crying. One boy shouted, "I don't believe you!" I felt mad. How could this happen to Jimmy?

Mending Hearts
When a school grieves

The counselor told us that all of our feelings are perfectly normal.

When someone dies it is okay to feel…
(circle the feeling you think is okay).

Has someone close to you died? How did or do you feel?

_____

_____

_____

_____

_____

_____

Mending Hearts
when a school grieves

The counselor told us that our sad feelings may last quite awhile. She said that it is okay for us to cry.

She said that we may feel angry at school. Keeping anger inside could cause us to break school rules.

Mending Hearts
When a school grieves

The counselor also explained that Jimmy died because of an accident. It was not our fault.

Children sometimes feel like they could have done something to prevent the death. They may think that if they had been kinder to their friend he would not have died. Do you feel this way?

Mending Hearts
When a school grieves

I looked at Jimmy's desk. I couldn't believe he wouldn't be coming back to school.

Mending Hearts
When a school grieves

The counselor told us that it is important to talk about your feelings. She told us we could talk to her anytime.

How are you feeling?

_____

_____

_____

_____

_____

Who else could you talk to? (Circle your answers)

Teacher

Principal

Parent

Friend

Minister

Grandparent

Aunt

Uncle

Talking to others sure helps you feel better!

Mending Hearts
When a school grieves

Then our teacher and counselor helped us make cards for Jimmy's family. That helped us feel better too!

What else could we do to feel better?
Making a memory book could help us remember the good times we had together (see page 42). Also, drawing or painting pictures could help us express our feelings. What else can you think of?

Mending Hearts
When a school grieves

The death of a special friend is hard on everyone! Remember that you are not alone. We can help each other get through this tough time.

Together, we will mend hearts!

Mending Hearts
When a school grieves

Mending Hearts

Group Counseling Sessions

Parental Permission Letter

You may use the letter below in it's entirety or edit to fit your needs.

Dear Parents:

I will be conducting a small counseling group for children who have experienced the death of a close family member. During the group sessions we will discuss feelings we have when we lose someone we love, ways to cope with our loss, and things we can do to feel better. The students will make a memory book with writings and drawings. The group will meet twice a week for three weeks.

If you would like for your child to participate, please sign the form below and return it to my office. If you have any questions, you can reach me at_____.

Sincerely,

School Counselor

- -

I give permission for my child,_____, to participate in small-group counseling sessions on grief.

Parent's signature_____ Date_____

Introductory Session: "Me Box"

Explain to the students that during group counseling sessions they will have a chance to share their experiences and feelings about the death of someone they love.   They will also learn to understand their feelings about death.

Discuss group rules:

1. We are good listeners when someone is talking.

2. We take turns talking by raising our hands.

3. We are considerate of other people's feelings.

4. Everyone participates in all the group activities.

Making a "Me Box"

1. Group members will make a "Me Box" using the outline on the following page. In each box draw:

   • Me

   • My pet

   • How I look when I'm sad

   • Someone I knew who died

2. Students will then introduce themselves using the "Me Box."

3. Have a group poster made, so that each "Me Box" can be glued on the poster with the child's name added under it.

Me Box

Me	My pet

How I look when I'm sad	Someone I knew who died

Mending Hearts
when a school grieves

My Feelings Are Okay

You may have lots of different feelings about the death of the person you loved. All of these feelings are normal and natural.

I have many feelings:

_____ happy

_____ sad

_____ hurt

_____ angry

Other feelings I have:

_____ scared

_____ guilty

_____ loved

_____ lonely

When I feel _____, I can _____.

Student may draw a picture below.

Counselor, you may want to hand out blank sheets for students to express additional feelings and draw additional pictures.

Mending Hearts
When a school grieves

Teddy Bear Feelings

Explain to the students that each person in the group will be given a chance to share their story and feelings about the person who died.

Discuss group rules for sharing:

1. Listen carefully by keeping their eyes on the person who is talking and staying quiet.

2. Remember to wait for your turn.

3. Be considerate of everyone's feelings.

4. Do not share what others say outside the group room.

The teddy bear is held by each student when it's his/her turn to speak. Ask students to begin by saying, "My name is _____, and this is my story…."

After all the students have shared, give each child an index card and ask them to write down something they learned about feelings during the sharing time.

Mending Hearts
when a school grieves

Memory Books

Memory books are a great tool to help students express their feelings and deal with their loss. On the following pages, you will find instructions and a template to help them memorialize their friend or loved one in a memory book.

Getting Started: Instructions for students

Memory books can be an important way to share your feelings with others about the person who died. Choose items from the following pages to create your own memory book. You may want to use lots of colored pencils, crayons, and markers to make your book colorful. Stickers, tissue paper, and cardboard cutouts can also be helpful. You may want to put the pages in a special binder or create a cover yourself.

After completing your memory book, be sure to share it with others!

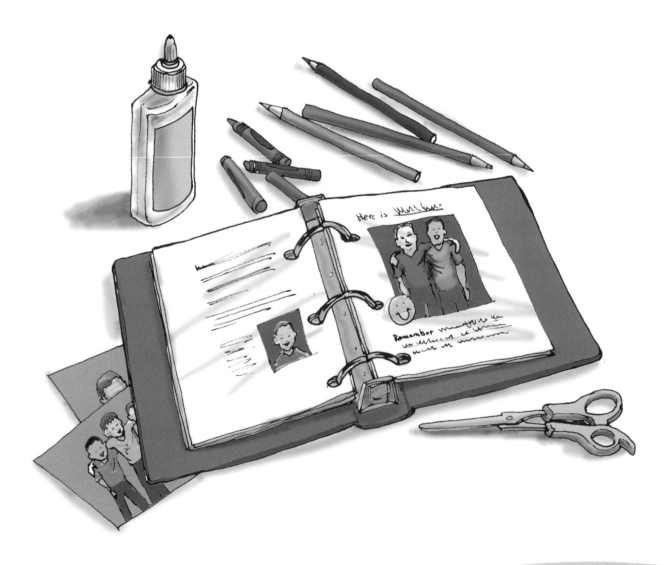

Mending Hearts
When a school grieves

My
Memory Book
about

_____

Write friend or loved one's name here

by

_____

date

_____

Mending Hearts
When a school grieves

Here is a picture of

_____.

Please paste or draw a picture below.

_____ was special to me!

I remember when I heard the news:

_____

_____

_____

_____

_____

_____

Mending Hearts
When a school grieves

Me and _____ at home.

Please paste or draw a picture below.

I remember:

_____

_____

_____

_____

_____

_____

_____

Me and _____ at school.

Please paste or draw a picture below.

I remember:

_____

_____

_____

_____

_____

_____

_____

Mending Hearts
When a school grieves

Me and _____
　　　　　　 having fun!

Please paste or draw a picture below.

I remember:

_____

_____

_____

_____

_____

_____

Mending Hearts
When a school grieves

My _____ was:

Draw a heart on the line next to each character trait he/she had.

____ cheerful   ____ funny

____ smart   ____ responsible

____ honest   ____ caring

____ hard worker   ____ thoughtful

____ kind   ____ respectful

____ sharing   ____ courageous

____ helpful   ____ organized

____ creative   ____ good citizen

Mending Hearts
When a school grieves

Things we enjoyed doing together were:

Draw a heart on the line next to activities you and your friend or loved one enjoyed.

____ being at school

____ cooking

____ playing together

____ jumping rope

____ celebrating a holiday

____ playing ball

____ eating a meal/snack

____ watching TV

____ going to the movies

____ being at home

____ playing a game

____ singing together

____ reading a book

____ taking vacation

____ making a craft

____ going to the beach

____ going to the mountains

____ other:_____

Mending Hearts

Activities for Individuals or Small Groups

I Got the Blues

All people have times when they feel really sad after losing someone they love. This sadness may come and go, and can last as long as a year. Remember that it is perfectly natural and normal to feel sad. Remember that it is okay to cry if you need to. Explore your feelings by completing the following.

Place a checkmark in the appropriate box.

I feel sad...

☐ 1 or 2 days a week   ☐ 3-5 days per week   ☐ most days

☐ for a short time   ☐ half the day   ☐ all day

☐ at school   ☐ at home   ☐ in my neighborhood

When I feel sad, I usually...

☐ ignore the feeling   ☐ talk to someone   ☐ cry

When I feel sad, people usually...

☐ share my sadness   ☐ listen   ☐ don't understand

When I feel sad, I think it would help me to...

_____

_____

_____

_____

_____

Mending Hearts
When a school grieves

Seeds of Hope

Death is part of life. Just as a person, plant, or animal is born; we know that a time will come for all living things to die. It can help us feel better to watch a plant grow and be reminded about how special life is.

Grow a plant!

You will need:

 A small pot or styrofoam cup

 Potting soil

 Plant seeds

 Water

Be sure to water your plant weekly. Watch your plant grow!

Mending Hearts
When a school grieves

Anger Awareness

All people experience times when they feel angry after losing someone they love. This anger may come and go at different times and with different people. Remember that it is perfectly natural and normal to feel angry. Explore your angry feelings by completing the following.

Place a checkmark in the appropriate box.

I feel angry...

☐ 1 or 2 days a week   ☐ 3-5 days per week   ☐ most days

☐ for a short time   ☐ half the day   ☐ all day

☐ at school   ☐ at home   ☐ in my neighborhood

When I feel angry, I usually...

☐ ignore the feeling   ☐ talk to someone   ☐ do something

When I feel angry, people usually...

☐ share my anger   ☐ listen   ☐ don't understand

When I feel angry, I think it would help me to...

_____

_____

_____

_____

Mending Hearts
When a school grieves

Things to Do with My Anger

When you feel angry, quite often it helps to do an activity to let the anger out. You may want to choose several activities from some of the ideas below.

Place a checkmark in the box next to the activities you think will help you deal with anger.

☐ Count to 10, slowly.

☐ Draw a picture.

☐ Write an "angry" letter.

☐ Talk to someone.

☐ Punch a pillow.

☐ Blow up a balloon and pop it.

☐ Stomp around or yell outside.

☐ Clean up my room.

☐ Wash the car.

☐ Make a list of everything that makes me mad.

☐ Go outside and pull weeds .

☐ Picture a stop sign in my head and take a time out.

☐ Make something out of play dough.

☐ Do an angry dance.

☐ Throw a bean bag.

☐ Take a shower.

☐ Listen to music.

☐ Play a sport.

☐ Think of a happy place.

Mending Hearts
When a school grieves

My Mood Picture

Have students make a picture that expresses their feelings about the person who died. Have them pick from the following symbols to make their picture.

Happy

Home

Mad

Sad

Afraid

Wishful

Out of control

Excited

School

Adapted in part from Fitzgerald, Helen. (1998). <u>Grief At School: A Manual for School Personnel.</u> Washington, D.C.: American Hospice Foundation.

Let's Make a Deal

Bargaining usually only lasts for very brief periods during the grieving process. An agreement with God or self is made that attempts to postpone facing the inevitable. You may feel guilty, believing that if you did something differently the loss would not have occurred.

Explore the stages of bargaining by completing the following:

If I had:

_____

_____

If only:

_____

_____

I'm sorry I:

_____

_____

I should have:

_____

_____

Face the facts:

_____ died, and I could not have prevented it.

Mending Hearts
when a school grieves

Books offer comfort and understanding to children suffering from the loss of a friend, relative, or pet. Reading to children about death can help you both through a difficult time.

Death in general

Ages 5-8:

Alley, Robert W. Sad Isn't Bad: A Good-Grief Guidebook for Kids Dealing With Loss. Abbey Press Printing and Publishing, 1998.

Ages 5 and up:

Buscaglia, Leo. The Fall of Freddie the Leaf. Henry Holt and Company, Inc., 2002.

Greenlee, Sharon. When Someone Dies. Atlanta: Peachtree Publishers, Ltd., 1993.

Death of parent

Ages 5-7:

Bunting, Eve. The Memory String. Houghton Mifflin Company, 2000.

Clifton, Lucille. Everett Anderson's Goodbye. Henry Holt & Company, Inc., 1990.

Thomas, Pat. I Miss You: A First Look at Death. Barron's Educational Series, Incorporated, 2001.

Whitehead, Ruth. The Mother Tree. New York: Seaburg Press, 1971.

Ages 8 and up:

Buck, Pearl S. The Big Wave. New York: The John Day Company. 1947.

LeShan, Eda. Learning to Say Good-bye: When a Parent Dies. New York: Macmillan Publishing Co., 1976.

Little, Jean. Mama's Going to Buy You a Mockingbird. Penguin Group, 1986.

Ages 10 and up:

Cleaver, Bill and Vera. Grover. Philadelphia: J.B. Lippincott Co., 1970.

Krementz, Jill. How It Feels When a Parent Dies. Knopf Publishers, 1988.

Continued on next page

Mending Hearts
When a school grieves

Ages 12 and up:

Creech, Sharon. <u>Walk Two Moons.</u>
HarperCollins Children's Books, 1996.

Death of grandparent

Ages 5-7:

Fassler, Joan. <u>My Grandpa Died Today.</u>
New York: Behavioral Publications, Inc., 1971.

Harris, Audrey. <u>Why Did He Die?</u>
Minneapolis, MN: Lerner Publications Company, 1965.

Haynes, Max. <u>Grandma's Gone to Live in the Stars.</u>
Albert Whitman Publishers, 2000.

Miles, Ruska. <u>Annie and the Old One.</u>
Boston: Little, Brown and Company, 1971.

Thomas, Jane Resh. <u>Saying Good-bye to Grandma.</u>
Houghton Mifflin Publishers, 1991.

Zolotow, Charlotte. <u>My Grandson Lew.</u>
New York: Harper and Row, 1974.

Ages 8 and up:

Henkes, Kevin. <u>Sun and Spoon.</u>
Penguin Putnam Books for Young Readers, 1998.

Jukes, Mavis. <u>Blackberries in the Dark.</u>
Knopf Publishers, 2002.

Ogel, Doris. <u>The Mulberry Music.</u>
New York: Harper and Row. 1971.

Death of sibling

Ages 8 and up:

Lee, Virginia. <u>The Magic Moth.</u>
New York: Seaburg Press, 1972.

Vogel, Isie Margret. <u>My Twin Sister Erika.</u>
New York: Harper and Row, 1976.

Continued on next page

Death of friend

Ages 5-7:

Bahr, Mary. If Nathan Were Here.
Michigan: William. B. Eerdmans Publishing Co., 2000.

Cohen, Janice. I Had a Friend Named Peter.
William Morrow and Company, Inc., 1995.

Stickney, Doris. Water Bugs and Dragonflies: Explaining Death to Young Children.
Pilgrim Press, 1997.

Ages 8 and up:

Smith, Doris B. A Taste of Blackberries.
New York: Thomas Y. Crowell, 1973.

Ages 10 and up:

Paterson, Katherine. Bridge to Terabithia.
New York: Harper Collins Publishers, 2004.

Death of pet

Ages 5-7:

Keller, Holly. Goodbye, Max.
HarperCollins Children's Books, 1987.

Rogers, Fred. When a Pet Dies.
Penguin Putnam Books for Young Readers, 1998.

Viorst, Judith. The Tenth Good Thing About Barney.
New York: Atheneum, 1971.

Warburg, Sandoval. Growing Time.
Boston: Houghton Mifflin Company, 1969.

Ages 8 and up:

Carrick, Carol. The Accident.
New York: Seaburg Press, 1976.

White, E. B. Charlotte's Web.
New York: Harper and Row, 1952.

Bibliography

Fitzgerald, Helen.
<u>Grief At School: A Manual for School Personnel.</u>
Washington, D.C.: American Hospice Foundation, 1998.

Kubler-Ross, E.
<u>On Death and Dying.</u>
NY: Touchstone, 1997.

<u>"Losing a Loved One: Helping Children Grieve."</u>
Parents (July 2001).

Wolfelt, Alan D.
<u>Healing The Grieving Heart: 100 Practical Ideas for Families, Friends, and Caregivers.</u>
Fort Collins, CO: Companion Press, 1998.